I Don't Care
How You Feel!
I Care
How You Think

Cognitive Therapy 2.0

John E. Christie MA, LPC

ISBN 978-1-0980-4796-2 (paperback)
ISBN 978-1-0980-4797-9 (digital)

Christian Faith Publishing, Inc.
832 Park Avenue
Meadville, PA 16335
www.christianfaithpublishing.com

Printed in the United States of America

CONTENTS

INTRODUCTION

I was like many when I was new to the counseling field—bright-eyed and bushy tailed, ready to save the world. However, as the years went by, I began to realize how many people didn't have the information they needed. In many cases, I wasn't helping people sort out their thinking. I was teaching them how to think.

Mental health is in the spotlight now, and people are scared. What's wrong with our world? There seems to be so many crazy people out there. Are mental health issues on the rise? Absolutely! But not for the reasons many promote.

It's not that people are more depressed or anxious. It's not like someone can hand you depression and you have to take it. We create it in our own heads. The issue is people are not being taught how their brains work, how they think. I believe if more people had the correct information, a majority of them would be able to control their minds, their thinking. I pray this book gives you that information.

Our world provides so much information, and so much of it can lead a person to focus on the wrong aspects of a situation. Even well-intended people, including therapists, can lead others down nonproductive alleys.

Much of what I hear in the area of self-help is still behaviorally based. Even though behavior can influence thinking, it is actually not the most effective path to change. Moreover, we receive tens of thousands of messages from society our whole lives. And unfortunately, most of those messages are 180 degrees from the truth. One of the lessons we learn from society is that what we are and what we own is most important.

We as people need to start to challenge the status quo messages. This guide will be a simple English explanation of how our brains work and provide a structured way to understand and control the way we think, feel, and act.

The amazing advances in neuroscience have considerably impacted our understanding of what happens in psychotherapy. If you are like most people, you would like to understand more about how some of these developments could be applied to your daily life.

In these pages, you will learn how the brain processes information. You will learn why the brain processes information. We will explore the true causational path of information and understand how better to control the process. We will examine how past events have contributed to the way we comprehend and perceive our world. You'll be given the insight to rewire your brain and update your thinking.

This book is meant to be a straight foward and practical resource which explains how to really change your brain for the better based on well-researched and grounded principles that worked for me and the thousands of people with whom I've worked. These concepts will help you actually use the idea of Neuroplasticity. Games and puzzles will help as well, but this theory will help you use it in an emotional way. It will aid you in controlling your own emotional health as well as help with relationships.

We will analyze where true self-confidence should come from and build a core belief system using those concepts. You will gain the information that will unlock the "secrets" that society says you can't change.

This will provide a mental framework to stay mindful and focused. It will serve as a gauge of progress as you work through the stages. We will be able to pinpoint exactly where we are in the process and keep things on course. It, along with the workbook, can also be used as a reference guide. Later, one can go back to the framework and concepts to refresh your ability to maintain mental health.

I've put this together, because God has allowed me in to see the inner working of people's minds. I have had over 15,000 sessions talking to people about their innermost world of thoughts. But what he has ultimately shown me is patterns. Distinct patterns in which people express what is happening in their lives, how they behave, how they feel, but ultimately, how they think!

Thinking is the most important thing we do; it controls everything. The brain controls our emotions and behaviors, and the mechanism it uses are thoughts. Thoughts control our energy, which is our space in the universe and ultimately is what connects us with God himself.

> It is the mark of an educated mind to be able to entertain a thought without accepting it.
>
> —Aristotle

1

WHY THOUGHTS MATTER

Cognitive Behavioral Therapy (CBT)

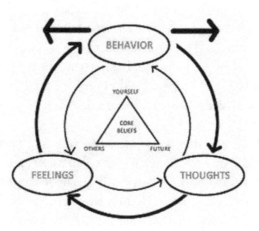

Image source from Wikipedia.

This diagram above is widely available on the internet, and honestly, I'm not a fan. I worry that all this model does is confuse the reader. There is no definition, and the diagram conveys that all things interact with everything else. The chart neither appears to show any order or discernible way to control the process. I fear this type of information turns people off to try to help themselves or even trust in counseling.

Unfortunately, these woefully inadequate examples are common in our society. Many books and Ted Talks have shortcomings in their advise. Either they use special terms and catchphrases to entice their audience and give the impression that you need that person and their information, because no one else seems to use the terms they use. Or worse yet, they espouse behavior change and how that is the key to mental health.

All this does is dilute the message and confuses the reader or listener on what it is they should be working on. When we hear phrases like "your attitude, focus, story, mindset, perception, even cognition," it doesn't address the primary problem. What is it exactly that people are supposed to change? What controls our story, mindset, or motivation? What are people supposed to monitor so we can determine the negative patterns and better control them?

They will tell you just to make time for yourself, get a pedicure, go on vacation, or go on a hike (these are quick fixes and don't address the underlying problem). Hence, they will not produce long-term positive results. They will claim that changing your behavior is the road to changing your life. I can get to the gym, but if all I'm thinking is how I hate to sweat, I'll never lose the weight. I need to and how embarrassing it is to be there; it is unlikely I'll sustain my behavior.

So in this book, I will try and keep things as succinct as possible. I will give you techniques with explanations that tell you how and why they will work. Our work will not be feelings based. I don't care how you feel! We will not ignore emotion. However, it will not be the focus.

We must look at the complete picture and decide to work on the *cause* of feelings. Certainly, we "feel" our feelings first, and it's the way our bodies are designed. We may have thousands of thoughts that make up a feeling, but the brain doesn't allow us to be conscious of them. It is unlikely that we would get anything done if we were constantly aware of every thought we had. However, it is imperative we understand more about our thinking.

> The wicked put up a bold front, but the upright
> give thought to their ways.
> —Proverbs 21:29 (NIV)

2

THINK! HOW THE BRAIN
PROCESSES INFORMATION

TEA (Thoughts, Emotions, Actions) is the first major concept that we must understand. The brain takes in information and processes it; it does this so fast that we hardly notice. However, it is the first internal action. The information doesn't go to your big toe or your liver; the information goes to your brain, and your brain thinks.

Information processing in the brain starts with input from various sensory organs, which help transform different physical stimuli, like touch, sound waves, heat, or photons of light into electrochemical signals.

Then feelings and chemicals are produced in the body to match the thoughts, which then lead to actions to further back up the thoughts. But thinking starts it all! So we must be more mindful and take a more active role in the process.

One of the reasons we must do this is that the brain is wired to protect, so it's kind of preprogrammed to think negatively. Negative thoughts do serve an important function! Negative thoughts keep us safe. Also, most of us have had experiences that have shaped how we think, some very traumatic. This trauma can add to negative thinking. Then add the messages we get from society of how the world is so dangerous, and one can see how we live in a more fear-based world.

We see the negative in any situation due to our mental filters. We can dwell on it and perceive the whole situation as negative.

Mental filters happen, for example, when you call your friend or husband insensitive and rude for not listening to you during dinner time while disregarding all other good things they did that day. It also happens when you are delivering an oral presentation and happen to see someone yawning. You instantly interpret it as a bad performance, completely disregarding the positive feedback you received.

All these make the brain think in a more negative perspective to protect itself and you. We have an additional hurdle, and the brain doesn't really want you messing around with it. Much like the electrical room in any major building that says "Do not enter! High voltage!" The brain is wired to work without conscious thought interfering with subconscious thought. However, left unchecked, the brain can get overwhelmingly negative. But as active, intelligent, and mindful people, we must break in and rewire what has shorted out.

Now, before the internal happenings of the mind, the person needs something to "react" to, and we will call these *events*. Anything can be an event for the brain. The drive to your office was an "event" in your life, so is going on a roller-coaster ride or having a child.

Some "events" are more important to the brain, but ultimately, they are all neutral and external until we think about them, until we assign value or an association to them. The brain assigns value and meaning to an object through thoughts; that is the first internal event.

Researchers have found that the brain can start to process value only eighty milliseconds after seeing an object. That is less than one-tenth of a second. It means that the brain is essentially figuring out if something is important to pay attention to or just junk while recognizing what it is based on history.

A pen might not elicit a lot of thoughts sitting on a table, because it doesn't mean a lot to you unless you need to write something. But if someone picked up that pen and held it so it was pointing out of their fist and started to run toward you, your brain wouldn't care that it's a pen any longer and would think of it as a weapon, and therefore, you have a completely different set of thoughts about it. In turn, your emotions and action would change, even though the pen didn't change its practical properties.

Our thoughts will determine whether we "like" (emotion) an event or not, and those feelings will determine whether or not we interact (action) with that event or not. If you have positive thoughts about a roller coaster (roller coasters are fun!), you will like them and, in turn, ride them. Indeed, once the system is active, then emotions and behavior have an impact on thoughts, but only after the initial thoughts have taken place.

TEA:

— Thoughts
— Emotions
— Actions

This is the true order of things. Thoughts control emotions, emotions control actions. Again, once the system is activated, then your emotions and actions influence future thinking, but not control; that's the crucial difference.

Your thoughts influence how you perceive events. If you receive an e-mail from your boss that says he or she would like to see you immediately, you may assume you will get fired. This is your brain attempting to protect you. Being fired might be the worst possible thing, so the brain prepares you. The subconscious mind thinks if it's something positive, then it doesn't have to prepare you for that.

If on the other hand you receive that same e-mail from your boss, one of your thoughts could be that you will be promoted or congratulated on a task or job well done. It is important to consider and reflect on the emotional thought filter you are looking at the world through. After that, you should reframe your thoughts and develop a more pragmatic and balanced view. Review both the positive and negative reasons an event could be happening. This will keep one emotion, such as anxiety, from dominating your perception.

And let's not get caught in the trap that *events* "cause." Events do not control thinking, except in rare, usually life-threatening situations. Obviously, no one should be making the case for positive life effects of heroine! However, think of everyday things such as roller coasters. They do not elicit the same response in everyone. Some people think positively about them, and some people think negatively of them. Just as not all people like chocolate ice-cream.

The following is a worksheet for your homework. Start to identify the four major themes. Do not feel you have to fill them out in order; often, we recognize feelings or behaviors before we understand the thoughts behind them.

> Set your minds on things above, not on earthly things.
>
> —Colossians 3:2 (NIV)

WORKSHEET 1

Identifying the four major themes

    Event:

    Thoughts:

    Emotion:

    Actions:

3

DIGGING DEEPER—SPECIFIC CATEGORIES OF THOUGHT

Thoughts are the cause of emotions and ultimately actions or behavior and understanding how we think will better help you control your brain.

Thoughts—In order for us to control our mental health, we must understand the types of thoughts we can have.

There are three dichotomies:

Negative vs. Positive

This is the classic pro/con list we have all done a thousand times.

For part of your brain, there's always something to protect against, and nothing is really quite right. In order to prepare you and keep you safe, it needs to know all the possible ways in which something can go wrong.

In contrast, part of your brain looks for the silver lining in apparent difficulties, hardships, and negative circumstances. This helps keep a positive and upbeat attitude and a good mood.

Keep in mind, the brain does both whether you like it or not. So let's not get caught in the argument of which is right but learn to entertain both possibilities.

Internal vs. External

The brain also cares how this "event" will affect you; that's internal and how this "event" will affect other people and things around you; those are external thoughts. This dichotomy may at first seem easy to understand; however, oftentimes, I see them get confused. A person may bring up an issue she or he has with their spouse. Oftentimes that spouse, before addressing the original problem, will bring up a problem they have with their mate. For example, one partner says, "I don't like that you're always coming home late from work."

Then the other replies, "Well, I don't like how much you drink." In these cases, rarely is anything accomplished.

Again, the goal isn't to decide which is right but to understand both.

Practical vs. Emotional

This dichotomy is a bit more complicated. "Events" also have practical and emotional aspects; these must always be known. This concept is crucial when doing couples counseling!

The brain always sees events having both or at least having the possibility of both. If someone tells me to lose weight, the practical part of that is true. I could stand to lose a few. However, my brain also contemplates if they had an emotional reason for saying that. In addition, it has two options, positive and negative. The positive one being they care about me and they want me to be healthy, and the negative one that they want to point out my flaws and embarrass me.

Even when I think about my car, there are both. Some of my thinking is practical. I want it to start and stop appropriately. However, I also want to "like" the color or the features. In this case, I've balanced my thinking so I can have a more thorough and mindful approach to buying a car. If someone leans to the practical, they are more likely to buy a car that gets good gas mileage and has a track record for not breaking down. If someone is an emotional thinker and doesn't care about practical concerns, that person will probably want an Italian car.

Eight Combinations

The three dichotomies, or six ways to think, make eight possible combinations. This is represented in the tree below. Once the brain thinks about something, it starts to break it down. This is similar to the body digesting food. It pulls it apart into its separate categories. Our job is to be mindful of the different ways it breaks it down instead of assuming the first reaction we have is the "right" one.

We must remember that the brain is negatively wired as its number one job is to keep you alive; if you die, it dies. Also, know your brain doesn't care what something is, only what it means, especially to you. Negative thoughts come first, and then if the brain determines the event isn't a threat, then more positive can come, and also more practical thought branches can be used.

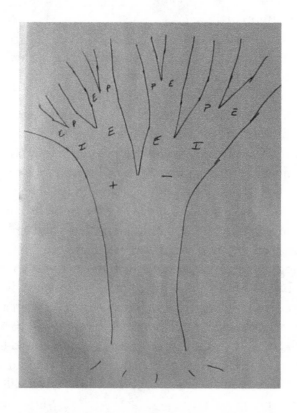

This tree above represents how the brain breaks down whatever it is thinking about. This representation is how all of them work. Even though we are all unique, our body digests food basically all the same, and our brain works on a very basic level in the same way.

This is an important concept in the work you'll be doing. Understand how your brain works, and you'll be able to control it. If you're able to control your brain, you tap into an energy that courses through the universe, the God particle; the energy is so complex that we barely understand the depth of it. In fact, I have found many people consciously and unconsciously avoid controlling their brain.

What these people are actually communicating is that they don't want to think! To me, this is the greatest tragedy of my time on this planet. This leads to so many of our problems in this society. We have a term now because some people see it and some people don't, and they are the sheeple. They take in the information they are given from an external source without any question or thought, and it becomes the way they think; they internalize it.

It's just easier that way, and this is happening in our news, government, schools, relationships, and homes. The people who do it like it because their thought world is disrupted by conflicting thoughts. People feeding you this potentially misleading information like it because they get their way without much struggle.

We are told a lie, and we soak it up, because then our thoughts are congruent with the "happy" thoughts we want to have, and we can avoid negative thoughts. I mean, hey, don't we all have enough negative thoughts about ourselves? Do I really want to also think negatively about a spouse that could be cheating or a company that is really ripping me off or question a government about policies, actions, or official narratives? No way! Too hard, too much work, too much thought!

And people who create these lies and distractions are all too happy to continue to make situations more and more complicated. They know the vast majority of people will take the lie, and many others will look suspicious but accept the thought as their own in time. Very few people still think for themselves, which is a real shame. For example, a recent survey done by Reuters reveals how a lot of Americans base their opposition or support to a particular political stance, not on the reliability of the public policy, but based on whether it comes with the strong backing of a favored political authority.

In a book written in 1930s, Hill wrote of his interview with the devil, that the enemy believes he had 98 percent of the people. Satan called these people Drifters, people who don't think for themselves! This was in the '30s! I don't believe that he has lost much of that percentage if any at all. I see this all the time. The parent who says they don't even want to know if their kids are doing drugs or having sex; the spouse who doesn't want to ask the tough questions about where someone was last night or who was on the phone.

It's many of us when we look at an event that doesn't seem logical but believe the commission's report or what is reported in the media as the whole truth. It is imperative we understand how our brain works, how and why it processes information (thinks). It's what separates us from the animals. It also allows us to communicate effectively; it allows us to learn and grow. These have all been examples of Cognitive Dissonance. Simply put, Cognitive Dissonance is the desire to reduce negative thoughts by accepting the thoughts of others i.e. letting others think for us!

Getting back to thoughts, society barely knows the depth of the power of the brain. The vibrational energy it produces and God has led me to study energy; thought energy. And now that he has shown me the tremendous and fantastic power of the brain, I am convinced it is the greatest form of energy in the universe if we can take the challenge of controlling and creating thought in ourselves, which is no small feat.

> Dear friends, this is now my second letter to you.
> I have written both of them as reminders to stim-
> ulate you to wholesome thinking.
> —2 Peter 3:1 (NIV)

4

THE HIERARCHY OF THOUGHT

Like many other social animals, human beings are status-conscious creatures. We are obsessed with hierarchy. This structure will give you the ability to rank and order the importance of thoughts. It also gives you the skill to determine true thoughts from lies. When the Bible talks about discernment, this is what it means! We are to have discernment in our thinking.

Let's look at each branch of thought and go through some examples.

Green Zone Thinking

Low Priority—Positive-External-Practical—Joe is good at math. So the brain says, "Great for Joe, no big deal for me."

Positive-External-Emotional—Joe is a good person. Matters more if Joe is in our life as he is not as much of a threat, and the brain can relax and not keep Joe on the radar.

Positive-Internal-Practical—I am good at math. More impactful because if math needs to get done, we can do it and we don't have to rely on Joe. This is self-sufficiency.

Positive-Internal-Emotional—I am a good person. This is the most important on the list and hardest to keep alive. Why? Although essential, it's positive and is not a danger. This branch of thinking keeps us in the growth mode, but more on this later.

This next group of thoughts all has something in common, negative and potential threats. Now the brain has picked up its antenna, and these thoughts will need more attention.

Yellow Zone Thinking

Negative-External-Practical—Joe is terrible at math. It is negative but not really a threat unless he is your accountant.

Negative-External-Emotional—Joe is a bad person. The brain certainly wants to pay attention as he could be a potential threat and will need to be thought about more.

Red Zone Thinking

Negative-Internal-Practical—Now we're getting hot. I am not good at math. I am not attractive. If the brain thinks you do not possess the skills necessary in life, high alert status can be initiated.

Negative-Internal-Emotional—I am not a good person. This has high potential for red-lining the car. If the brain thinks you suck on an emotional scale, then you will suck in all areas of your life, not just math or weight. The mind can now go into a hyper-sensitive fear mode in the long term, general sense, seeing everything as a threat.

Remember, though, I listed Green Zone to Red Zone; it's the Red Zone thoughts that come first. We have to work through the red thoughts to allow the brain to rest on the green. As we work together, you'll get better at identifying the different thoughts and then choosing which thoughts to devote energy. A good system for dealing with the Red Zone is essential if we want to live in the Green Zone.

For by the grace given me I say to every one of you:

Do not think of yourself more highly than you ought, but rather think of yourself with sober judgment, in accordance with the faith God has distributed to each of you.

—Romans 12:3 (NIV)

5

THE PROBLEM OF AVOIDANCE (FEAR VS. GROWTH MODE)

When we experience uncomfortable or unpleasant emotions, thoughts, or sensations, there's usually a natural tendency to avoid most of these uncomfortable or unpleasant experiences, sometimes at any cost. This is known as experiential avoidance. And the irony is that this avoidance can maintain psychological distress.

Experiential avoidance often prevents humans from being accepting of as well as present to our various inner reactions. This is usually problematic in various respects. As it detaches us from feeling, avoidance can interfere with the very function of our emotional response.

Avoidance is when we fail to let our brain fully process (or think about) an event. We prevent or avoid in various ways, such as drugs, sleep, and work, etc. As we discussed, the brain's first job is to determine a threat or be in fear mode. If we are able to stay in the red zone long enough, the brain will move past this fear mode response and be able to get to the green zone or growth mode response.

One of the main issues I see in people is they start to let the brain think/process an event, and it gets hard; really hard. We can then start to think that the hard part will never end or it's too much for us to handle, and then we bail. We don't allow enough time for the brain to get to know the situation isn't really a threat or even how it might be a positive thing. It's this cycle of trying and bailing that is creating a generation of snowflakes.

However, we can be patient to let the brain determines the event isn't a threat or no longer a threat. It can proceed to the positive branches or growth mode. This allows for thinking/processing, like "making the best of the situation;" it gives us perspective such as "It could have been worse;" "I should consider myself fortunate x happened the way it did." It also allows for the current processing of information. Within the positive branches, there are internal, external, practical, and emotional branches. More on the specifics later.

The brain does not want to process new information or not process it well if it is in fear mode. Some people refuse to look at all the thoughts about an event, because the negative aspects overwhelm them. So they need to ignore them so that the brain can get back into the growth mode. This is the unhealthy way to get the brain back to growth mode. It is usually short-lived and in a narrow scope of one's life.

When we stop the brain from processing negative thoughts that are so overwhelming, we have short-term relief, but it doesn't really accomplish anything. This is because negative thoughts are still there the next day, and negative situations continue to happen without being addressed.

This is a false positive way to live, a head in the clouds mentality. However, some people prefer this method to one of the alternatives. And those are people who truly live in fear. With so many negative thoughts, we train the brain only to see the negative or to stop at the negative and get stuck in the fear mode.

Part of the subconscious mind's job is to look into the environment for proof of the belief system. So if we are in fear mode, and since everything has some negative to it, one can see a dangerous combination. We will see and think negative in everything and perpetuate our fear.

In every threatening or stressful situation, our brain starts to log details and add warning labels. You might not notice this at the time. This is because you are too busy handling the situation. However, later when you encounter a similar detail to that stressful or threatening situation, you will find yourself with a racing heart and sweaty palms. However, being mindful of all the ways to think about a situation allows us to be meta-cognitive of the effects and then combat them.

For example, if a person has almost drowned at the age of eight, it is unlikely for that child to have the meta awareness that they may have an issue with water later in life. And I'm not sure about you, but I was left with my trauma as a child to deal with on my own. No one ever came up to me and said, "Hey, John, you're going to have issues with water later in life. You should be aware of that." So we develop a belief structure about life, and many of us are unaware of how that foundation was constructed.

We also train our brain to think to turn to behavior to fix it. This includes, sleep, drugs, work, and focusing on others, etc. As hard as it is, we must work with and train our brain to "process" through the thought tree; we cannot leave that side of the tree without fruit devoid of any foliage.

We must get back to growth mode and present and future-oriented thinking most effectively and appropriately possible. We must take the challenge to take back our brains and think for ourselves. We must decide if our fear-based negative thinking is real. Is it based on fact or a "feeling?" Or worse yet, what someone else said about us? When we get to those more reality-based thoughts, it produces emotions of relief, openness, appreciation, and love, etc., then produces behavior or actions that show growth.

> How precious to me are your thoughts, God!
> How vast is the sum of them!
> —Psalm 139:17 (NIV)

6

THE BIOLOGICAL PROCESS

The amygdala is your brain's bodyguard and is always looking for threats. The prefrontal cortex is responsible for logic, reasoning, and executive function. The hypothalamus is the body's equalizer. The sympathetic nervous system regulates how our muscles respond.

When the information from your senses enters the body, it is directed to the brain. The first stop is the amygdala. If the amygdala decides an event is a threat, then this actively stunts the activity of the prefrontal cortex, resulting in less blood flow and less electrical activity. The amygdala helps us in identifying threats in our environment. In case threats are present, it initiates a "fight or flight" response

It's the brain's way of protecting itself. It's not time to analyze whether the knife is sharp; it's only time to decide to fight or run. The real problem is that if we have trained the brain to see almost everything as a threat, we then live in the fear mode, which produces chronic anxiety, anger, and/or depression.

This then results in negative actions or behavior, such as crying, avoidant behavior, and drinking, etc. The brain thinks it's in danger, so it makes the hypothalamus produce more chemicals, like cortisol and adrenaline, which are fine in the short-term but massively detrimental in the long run. Long-term increased adrenaline and cortisol creates muscle tension and ailments, like ulcers.

The hypothalamus is similar to a command center in many ways. This part of your brain communicates with the rest of your body via the autonomic nervous system. This system regulates many involuntary body functions, like blood pressure, breathing, heartbeat, and the constriction or dilation of important blood vessels as well as the airways in your lungs.

Filters

Finally, all these systems will eventually affect our "filters." This is crucial. Part of the brain's job is to find evidence in the environment of the person's belief system. And when we are in fear mode, the brain will look for things to be fearful of. It can start to perceive the world as a dangerous place.

We will only see negative when both positive and negative exist. It needs to as you are in danger, and it needs to protect you. This can manifest itself in many ways, small ways, such as being afraid of spiders. This can happen in much broader ways, such as thinking life is dangerous and threatening or that life or you are worthless.

Knowing and Setting your Filters

This concept uses the information gathered in the previous work to understand how patterns in your thinking have affected your filters. Your brain filters information as it comes in and will give you the relevant information, and that relevant information is based on the way you think.

To demonstrate how the filter works, you can picture the following situation: You're sitting at a very busy cafe or local restaurant and having a deep conversation with an individual across from you. Note that you can clearly hear everything which is going on in the room. For example, the soundwaves are reaching your ear; however, your brain filter is activated and filters away all the irrelevant noise. This allows you to only hear what the individual sitting in front of you is saying. Also, keep in mind that this is the exact same reason you are able to read a book or magazine while the television is on. Your sub-conscious brain simply "turns off" the sound coming from the television.

If you think negatively and are in the fear mode, your brain must pay more attention to the negative, whether it is risks, effects, outcomes, or consequences. This helps protect you. However, since everything has negative aspects, this way of thinking and filtering information will only lead to thinking about things in an overarching negative way, the positive will be there but muted in the background or shadows.

Imagine you are standing on a subway platform and peering into a big crowd of individuals waiting alongside you. Because of the filter, your attentional spotlight is often dragged automatically toward the negative facial expressions, and you ignore the positive ones. This is why everyone appears to be a bit upset, and all of a sudden, things seem darker and gloomier overall.

Also, on your ride home, once all of the stops have passed, except yours, a burly man wearing a black hoodie who is sitting near you suddenly reaches into his jacket pocket. This captures your attention, and you may think he was reaching for a knife or gun. Fortunately, it was only a mobile phone, but it forces you to think hard about how you may have not been lucky.

Because your threat bias tends to filter out all of the positive aspects and lets in just the negative, fear and worry flow through your cognitive system. This results in an exceedingly threat-conscious assessment of the subway environment. The entire experience strengthens the perception that the subway is a very dangerous place and is full of questionable characters.

This negative filter perception has the power to shape our broader worldviews and affect our politics and ideologies thereby influencing us to see the world and our lives as vastly negative and threatening.

> So I tell you this, and insist on it in the Lord, that
> you must no longer live as the Gentiles do, in the
> futility of their thinking.
> —Ephesians 4:17 (NIV)

7

THE REAL WORK BEGINS

Stage 1—Understanding Where Negative Thinking Comes From

Now that you know all the different types of thinking, we are going to plug in your experiences and effects into the thought tree and see how events have impacted your thinking. This is where the real work begins and what keeps a lot of people out of therapy. This is where the concepts meet you head on. It's going over our trauma. Now, a word on trauma. This is a loaded word, and a lot of people will define it in many ways.

Trauma is your response to any terrible event, such as an accident, natural disaster, or rape. Shock and denial are common immediately after the terrible event. Psychological trauma is likely to leave you struggling with many upsetting memories, emotions, that simply won't go away. It may also leave you feeling disconnected, numb, and unable to trust other people.

So for our use, we will say it is any situation which had a negative impact on your thinking. Yes, I realize there are probably so many situations you have been in where you won't be able to recall them all. I am not interested in all of them. The situations I am after are the ones either you know well or, given some time, will come up with all on its own.

These are the ones that have affected your negative internal emotional thoughts. All the brain needs is a little push in the right direction and time, and you will have plenty of memories to talk about.

This is not to say we won't be talking about any current issues that you are having. A thorough conversation about the current problem, including time and intensity, is paramount. However, we will also want to know if there was a triggering event or events and if there is any part of the situation that has historical significance that might have made it a trigger. For example, seeing an individual related to the trauma can set off a trauma reaction. Similarly, some sensations, like pain, are triggers. So for a survivor of an assault, a touch on a specific body part might lead to a flashback.

And that is why much of Stage 1 is of the past and how it has affected how we think of the present. The trauma, including the secrets we carry, is the major factor in how we view or think about our world today. It starts very young in creating patterns for the "branches" the brain gets accustomed to using. Remember, the brain wants and needs to be very efficient, so the faster it can categorize something, the better.

And since the brain wants to protect you, it is willing to think of things as a threat. It is the habitual categorization of things as a threat, or negative that impacts our perspective on the present and the future. These neuro-pathways create meaning, messages, and associations. They lay the foundations of *how* we think.

As we go through the past trauma and understand how it affects thinking through the eight branches of thought, we then need to decide what to keep and what to throw away, which I sometimes call "cleaning out the attic."

We will determine if what we have learned about the other person, situation, life, ourselves is truth or a lie. The most important of the branches is how the past has influenced how we emotionally think of ourselves. This is the one we focus on and work to change. The wonderful thing about being a human being is that we can choose our thoughts. We have been given the power of metacognition, and too many of us are not using it.

We can't choose to think it didn't happen and still be congruent with reality. We also can't think ourselves as being ten feet tall. However, we can choose to think about whatever we want emotionally about ourselves, and this goes for negative and positive. If we think something happened because we are "less than" or worthless, then that is the definition the brain will go with. It's actually an easy answer for the brain. The brain can't ever really know what the motivation was for another person, so the brain can default to a "your fault" mentality.

The issue is that "your fault" mentality will have severe consequences in how we think about any future event. For example, if someone thinks they are worthless, they are more likely to expect or even allow someone else to treat them in a worthless way, which is why we like to go back as far as possible to ferret out the original negative turn. We don't want to get caught in working on a trauma when that was caused by an already corrupted negative thought pattern.

However, this is not always possible with something like pre-memory abuse. Often, these babies who are abused or neglected are wired in this negative way but have no way of remembering the trauma. Good news, we don't need stage one to progress to stage two. It is certainly ideal if we can look into the past and see the original sin, but we can work with whatever one remembers, even if it isn't the first trauma that person had been through.

At the time of most traumatic events, your mind makes several associations with the sights, feelings, sounds, taste, smells, and touch linked with the trauma. Later on, similar sensations can trigger a memory of that event. Although some individuals first remember their past traumatic events during therapy, a lot of people begin having these traumatic memories outside therapy.

Here is a word on negative thoughts. As we talked about in the beginning, negative thoughts have an essential purpose. They keep us safe. I would never want a client not to have negative thoughts. It's impossible anyway; the amygdala makes sure of that. Negative thoughts not only keep us safe; they are suitable for accountability and self-improvement.

What we need is balance and perspective. We as Americans seem to think if a little negative thinking is good, then we should have a whole bunch of it! But that only ends up being a self-defeating exercise and does not help with self-improvement.

We human beings also love being hypocritical. Many of the wonderful rules and advice we have for others do not apply to ourselves. So many people come in and give their sisters, brothers, and neighbors the best advice and empathy one could provide, but when it comes to supplying that for themselves, it is long gone, replaced with damnation, scorn, and contempt. I ask almost every client, "If someone else talked to you the same way you talk to yourself, would you still be their friend?" And almost unanimously, they say no.

Another concept we must recognize is that negative thoughts often are very true at times. The little girl who didn't want to be touched by the neighbor was in danger. And all the negative thoughts she had about the situation and externally about her abuser were true. However, it's the negative thoughts the little girl developed about herself that are the enemy here.

So one of the first concepts is that the thoughts were relevant and real; they are just not relevant anymore. The little girl who thought she was powerless is no longer a little girl and can protect herself as an adult. This is why we are not digging around the past to change the past or to blame anyone. But we do need to see how it affected thinking.

Forgiveness

Now, once you have that list, you have a decision to make. Are you going to continue to believe those words? Are they based on fact? Have you mistakenly taken an event and interpreted a negative internal emotional meaning from it? Have you been abused or done a negative thing to another and thought you're a terrible person, less than or worthless?

Has someone told you that you were worthless? Well, let me give you an example and see what you think. I have a ten-year-old female client who thinks she is garbage and useless because she was abused. The abuse was real, but would you tell her that her negative internal emotional thoughts of worthlessness were also true? And the unanimous answer is no! And sorry, you have to follow the same rules. If she isn't worthless, neither can you be for the trauma you've had. It's the hypocrisy trap.

Your negative internal emotional thoughts (self-talk, script, story). When you are negative, what are the things you say to yourself (think)? Do you know what events those thoughts were born from?

> Brothers and sisters, stop thinking like children. In regard to evil be infants, but in your thinking be adults.
> —1 Corinthians 14:20 (NIV)

8

Your Emotional Toolbox

Stage 2

This is the stage where we get to decide what to think. Not just what we think about ourselves, which is the most important, but what we think of how we treat other people and other things around us, and even the negative events that are an inevitable part of our future.

The stage can be a real challenge for people. Deciding what to think is a foreign concept for some people, let alone positive emotional self-thoughts. Much of our self-talk is often rational and reasonable—"I better do some thorough preparation for the math exam;" or "I am really looking forward to the basketball game." That being said, some of our self-talk is certainly negative, self-defeating, or unrealistic—"I am going to flunk for sure;" or "I did not play well! I am hopeless."

Society doesn't really teach us how to think for ourselves. It only seems to want us to take in information and accept it without questioning it. But as so many societal messages are, this message is just as untrue as most of the others.

Positive thinking does not mean that you should keep your head in the sand and simply ignore life's challenging or less pleasant situations. Positive thinking simply means you approach challenges, problems, and unpleasantness in a more productive way. You don't always have to think the best will happen, but we also don't always have to think the worst. It's about balance!

If you're a believer, this stage of therapy will be based on what God thinks about you. If you're not so religious, then think of it as an emotional resume or an emotional toolbox to help with the challenges of life. It will allow you to have at the ready a foundation for you to handle and keep your thoughts focused when negative things are abundant in your life.

It can also propel you to greater heights when things are good. It gives what society likes to call confidence! But unlike society that seems to say your confidence should be in material things, this list will be based on your emotional qualities.

More specifically, it is the one branch that is Positive Internal and Emotional. As you can imagine, if someone said that they were feeling confident this week and they said it was because they just bought a new Mercedes Benz, we might think that is a bad answer. However, if you were asked why you seem so confident this week and you said because you believe that you are a loving, caring, generous, positive, and relaxed person, you might be inclined to think that it is a very good answer.

Another good example is someone in an interview. Although being able to type ninety words a minute is a fantastic skill, it doesn't tell me much about the character of the person. This is why an interviewer or an interviewee should spend some time on their emotional qualities as these qualities are transferable from one task to another.

I don't take my typing skills when I'm filing, but I do take my loving, caring, positive, and relaxed mindset to file or answer a phone than any other task that might be asked about. This is what I believe an interviewer should be looking for as well as just the skills to do the job.

There are even more reasons why this is so important and advantageous to learn. First, because these qualities are internal, the only person who controls the level of these characteristics is the person themselves.

No one else has the power to turn off my happiness. If someone is mean to me, it is my choice to lower my level of happiness. The only exception to this rule is when we're talking about physical harm. I do not suggest that someone continues to think happy or nice or positive thoughts when faced with imminent physical danger; that is a different story, and different skills need to be used.

However, I have found that in the vast majority of people's lives, they are not faced with such decisions. No one has tried to kill me in years! The second reason why this is so important is that emotions are infinite. If your happiness is so overflowing and you think that it spells out to somebody else and they are happy as a result, you don't lose any.

That doesn't work in the practical world. If I give someone 100 dollars, I have 100 less in my account. However, if I were to be loving to people all day, I can still come home and be loving. I don't run out of that! I enjoy working in areas that I have full control, and my resources are infinite. And because these qualities are infinite, if you see an emotional quality in someone else, you are allowed to have it. I have yet to talk to somebody who has mentioned an emotional quality they saw in someone else but they were not allowed to have.

No one has ever told me that God has come down from the heaven and said that they could only be a three out of ten on the happiness scale. It is just not how God sets it up. If you are a believer, this list is based on what God thinks about you. I have never read in the Bible that God thinks of me, or wants me to think of myself, as an angry, jealous, spiteful, mean, malicious person.

Of course, I have the capacity to be those things, but I don't think those thoughts are the foundation. God is our heavenly Father, and much like a father, our thinking toward our children should be loving and caring, and we want that for our kids. Not only to think these things but believe these things and hold them close.

Also remember this is not who you are today. This is not a list that needs to be true today. In fact, the person you are right now is history. The person we are talking about is gone. So if we try to build this list from the current you, we will get nowhere. This is a list you are building for the "six months from now" you. Giving a goal of six months from now helps your amygdala and your whole limbic system not freak out.

The current you has basically gone already. Once we start talking about the current you within a second or two, that you is in the past, so we must always be thinking and planning for the person you will become and not the person you are.

What we are doing here is making a list of emotional goals. The goals of emotional wellness often include things that help keep you mentally healthy so that you may live your life as a thought-based person without being unduly controlled by your emotions.

So many of us are willing and even want to make goals we don't understand that we're only making practical goals. And yes, if you want to make more money or buy a new house, I think those goals are wonderful but ultimately meaningless in the world of emotional thought.

Anyone can still be massively negative with money or on a vacation. We must be more conscientious about deeper levels of thought and holding yourself to a higher standard, and this is what I call the emotional toolbox; this is what we are working on. I am not making fun of practical goals; they are critical. They are just not the most important goals you can make. They're not even the most crucial part of life. Also, keep in mind societal messages; they will tell you the practical goals outweigh emotional goals. What I am talking about here is basically Identity Theory and whether or not you're going to put your identity in your things, the "what" you are or your emotional core, the "who" you are.

What you are building is the foundation for your confidence. You will now have an answer when people ask you how you feel, why you seem so confident why things are going well in your life. And you will have an answer when people ask how you're going to handle this negative thing that is going on in your life. You will have an answer for every question.

Now to work, you must build a list that is positive internal and emotional, basically a list of adjectives of who you are, what foundation you are going to hold yourself accountable to, and how you would like to be described. There is a list on a later page of words that can help you with this task. And since these characteristics are infinite, you can choose any of the words that you want.

Here's a word about appropriate negative thoughts and false positives. There are some thoughts that are negative, but they keep us in balance. For example, thoughts such as "I'm not perfect." But even these appropriate negative thoughts have to be held in check or they can get out of control.

And there are thoughts that seem positive but are not! For example, a good mom worries about her children. A reasonable person puts others' emotional and/or practical needs above their own. There are more examples of societal messages which need to be scrutinized before we adopt them.

How would you like to be described?
Positive, internal, and emotionally based.

> All of us, then, who are mature should take such
> a view of things. And if on some point you think
> differently, that too God will make clear to you.
> —Philippians 3:15 (NIV)

9

THE HARDEST PART

Stage 3—Activating the Subconscious Mind

This is the hardest stage of therapy. This is the stage where we need to get the subconscious mind on board. And to get this happening, conscious thought is required. This is not an easy task; the subconscious mind does not want your input as it works on an independent basis, monitoring the environment, and backing up your belief system. Keeping you safe is its number one goal.

Your subconscious mind consistently filters and brings to your attention stimuli and information that tend to affirm your preexisting beliefs. It is called confirmation bias. Your subconscious mind also presents you with repeated impulses and thoughts that mirror and mimic that which you have done in the past.

We must override the system; we must get in there and rewire this part of the brain. Another good way to think about it is to update the brain. In computers, I'm guessing the best way to go is to have the most updated operating system. So working with Windows 2.0 in 2018 probably won't get you very far. And this is true of the brain if we get triggered when we're thirty-four and go back to thinking as if we were an eight-year-old; note that that is not the most updated version of thinking.

I used to believe in the tooth fairy, but since then, I have received information to help change my thinking. I have updated my thinking, and it's more congruent with reality. I am happy I did so, and I'm sure it would seem more than weird if a forty-nine-year-old still had a lot of thought life dedicated to the tooth fairy. I want you to have the most updated version of emotional thinking that you can have about yourself.

You could achieve whatever you would like in life, provided you know exactly how to program as well as activate your subconscious brain the right way.

Now that you have your list, it's time to start training the brain. More specifically, the subconscious mind; however, we must use the correct language to communicate with the subconscious mind. And that is not words; words are way too slow for the subconscious mind.

The first important step in creating a dramatic change in your life isn't actually believing that it is possible; it is being willing and open to see if it's possible.

We will be using visualization or planting as I like to call it as it is much like planting a seed for a tree. It takes a long time to see things grow and come to fruition. Every year, a farmer plants seeds, and through extensive hard work, they sprout, and eventually, plants grow into maturity.

One of the skills is to imagine a situation in the future that would normally cause you to think negatively. Therefore, it will cause anxiety, and then beyond that, if the level of anxiety is high enough, it would actually affect your behavior or your actions.

We want to imagine the scenario but not be so concerned with the external forces involved. Rather, only hold onto the thought of how you are going to be in the given situation as you already have the list of your toolbox and how you are now going to handle things.

You can imagine that situation and how you will handle it according to the list you developed. I know, of course, you may not use all the characteristics you have listed. However, you should know which ones to pull out for a given situation.

The second task is to imagine the same situation going poorly externally but remembering it's the externals that might go poorly in the situation and that you remain constant. The same list, the same tools that you pull out of your toolbox, apply when the situation goes wonderfully or when the situation goes down the toilet, but you remain the same.

Example: A birthday party for a child is a great example. I want someone to spend a small amount of time imagining the cake gets dropped, food is cold, or something else goes wrong with that person. It could be the mom or dad who remains calm, loving, positive, humorous, and caring, etc. in the scenario.

This is the accurate measure of a person. It's not just how we handle positive things, the true measure is how we handle negative things. We can't always expect everything to go well, and if things go well, then they will be fine. We must be strong enough to have things go awry in our lives and still remain constant, solid, balanced, and confident thinkers.

Benefits of this exercise are both short-term and long-term. If you spent five minutes thinking about a situation and how you're going to handle it, well, it is five minutes that you spent positively thinking about yourself, and the brain loves that.

For long-term benefits, this role playing exercise trains your brain to think more positively about yourself in situations more often. This is ultimately the energy we want to tap into. We learn to rewire and restructure the brain to think about things in a different way, a more confident way.

Another way of thinking about this is living inside out. No longer do outside forces have control over your thoughts or emotions. And they certainly wouldn't influence your actions. Live inside out! Let your real desired nature show. Don't absorb the negative external emotional atmosphere.

Do not allow other people's negative attitudes and fears cast a shadow of a doubt. Note that the way individuals respond to news of your success would tell you how they're actually doing in their lives. For example, if you announce the news of your engagement or marriage; people who're in happy marriages would be elated for you. On the other hand, people who're not happy in their marriages would warn you that it's difficult, so you should fully enjoy your remaining time as "single" individuals.

If you are dealing with the issues most people are, you will not be putting yourself in danger if you continue to be caring, positive, and assertive. However, as a caveat, if you think you are in a dangerous situation, you should remove yourself and readdress the situation at a more appropriate time.

Remember, we are activating the brain on two levels—consciously with directed thinking, and subconsciously by reinforcing the concept of safety. It signals to the brain that if we can "frivolously" think of positive things, we must not be in real imminent danger.

This will teach the subconscious mind and the limbic system to relax and allow more room for positive thinking. It will make your prefrontal cortex more easily accessible.

Please remember that this process is laborious. In fact, the hardest thing I think we can do is do the job we can undertake. Controlling a nine-pound lump of cholesterol that we really don't understand is no easy task. The fact that we don't know how it works certainly doesn't show us how it works and makes things even more complicated.

Therefore, I will need you to think of this task, much like that of a farmer. A farmer has to put in a ton of work over several months to even eat one ear of corn. So too will be your task. A lot of thought work must be done to rid the mind of old thoughts that have almost poisoned it. Only then can you reap the harvest with absolute dedication.

Slowly, you will see sprouts of the work you do. We will highlight these and gain momentum toward changes in emotion and actions. I implore you to stay committed; you can and will see how this system helps you appropriately control your life.

> Repent at my rebuke!
> Then I will pour out my thoughts to you, I
> will make known to you my teachings.
> —Proverbs 1:23 (NIV)

10

THE WORK AND
MORE CONCEPTS

If we learn to steer our thinking, control it and, yes, even manip-
ulate it, we can harness the energy needed to do almost anything.
Certainly, anything that the average person wants to manifest should
be attainable.

For example, when you're drawing a picture, you do not let it
simply become whatever it happens to become. Rather, you consciously direct all of your artistic talents to make the picture look
exactly like you want it to be. Keep in mind that the same applies to
your life, with your thoughts being the paintbrush.

Simply allowing random thoughts to dominate your mind and
hoping to have something great come out is akin to drawing with no
direction or effort and hoping to get a great-looking painting in the
end.

You should steer your life carefully with conscious purpose.
You can do this by focusing your thoughts on what you really want
instead of dwelling on what you do not want. You should think over
and over the type of thoughts you would like to dominate your life.

We must learn not only to balance our thinking but also look
for those positive truths that are there. This helps us be adaptable.
We must be mindful of the attacks as they can come from every-
where. When I say attacks, I mean negative thoughts: "This isn't for
me;" It only works for a little while."

Learn to be effort driven and not result oriented. Society wants us to think the most important part of life is the result. But the concept is backward as much of societal messages are. We must rethink that concept and realize it's the effort in today's world that matters most.

Hundreds of years ago, I am sure that was not the case. We lived in much more practical situations where the result was more important, because your literal life was at stake. Today, effort is far more important than the result. In addition, I would posit that we are vastly more successful in reaching our practical goals when we attempt to get them, already having our emotional goals in order.

Whether it is easy or hard, through working on thoughts, it's imperative that you recognize in what circumstances and with whom these skills are easy and when they are hard to use. This will give us a wealth of information about our patterns and triggers.

> Finally, brothers and sisters, whatever is true, whatever is noble, whatever is right, whatever is pure, whatever is lovely, whatever is admirable— if anything is excellent or praiseworthy—think about such things.
> —Philippians 4:8 (NIV)

11

BENEFITS OF THINKING

Effects/Why Should We Do This?

So why should we do this? Let's go over the advantages of controlling your own thinking. In these dynamic times of fast media as well as ever-growing Internet, most of us are under so many different external influences that it may be hard to know when we're thinking for ourselves.

There are many benefits of controlling your own thinking. For one, it allows you to live "inside out." And what I mean by that is linked to what I talked about society wanting you to only take in information.

I encourage people to develop internal thinking and live according to that thinking rather than just the information that is coming into you. To just react, to think that outside events do control you and control your thinking and that you can't think of any other way based on the situation, these are societal messages.

You are now the gatekeeper of information. You will be able to listen to anyone and their thoughts without automatically accepting them as your own. Some people will say that this is a weak way to live. However, it is not the weak way to run your life; it is actually far more powerful. This allows for original thought and not only consistency in your own thinking but your emotions and your behavior.

This, to me, is true empowerment. You will have power over your life. No longer will outside situations cause you to think a certain way; that information will come into you, and you will consciously decide what to think about it and how to respond rather than being reactive. This teaches you to be proactive in your thoughts and consistent in your emotions and your behavior.

Being proactive is about taking full responsibility for your life. Note that you just cannot keep blaming each and everything on your parents and grandparents. Also, proactive individuals recognize and understand that they're "response-able." This is why they do not blame circumstances, genetics, conditions, or their conditioning for their behavior. Also, they recognize that they choose their behavior, through their thinking.

On the other hand, reactive people are usually affected by their immediate physical environment. As a result, they often find various external sources to blame for their behavior. For example, if the weather is nice, they will feel great. In contrast, if it is not, it affects their performance and attitude, and they blame it.

However, you can stop being reactive. For example, in case you feel upset and angry with someone before you do or say something you may later regret, you should take a deep breath and then slowly count to ten. In a majority of circumstances, by the time you will reach ten, you will have given your brain time to figure out a much better way to communicate the issue. This will help you reduce the problem instead of escalating it. And if you are still upset after you have counted to ten, take some time out if it is possible, and then revisit the issue later. This will help you slowly and methodically go through your "tree," balance your thinking, and choose the branch of thought that makes the most sense and aligns yourself with truth. This is the purpose of behavioral advise like counting to ten, it gives your brain time to think!

Another benefit is that it makes you bulletproof, as I like to say. Although someone may not like the decision you have made, they cannot argue in the manner in which you made it. You have that already; you know you've made the decision in a loving, caring, generous, and positive way. You will now know the difference between them not liking what you did or said and not liking you. It makes you a good thinker and communicator in confrontation.

This also gives you an amazing amount of indirect control. People always want and overestimate direct control. The ability to simply tell someone what to do, how to think or feel, means a lot to them. Perhaps one of the deepest needs people have is a sense of control. When they feel out of control, they often experience an uncomfortable and powerful tension between the evidence of inadequate control and need for control.

Even the people we usually consider non-controlling are still pretty much controllers. This is because, in a sense, they want to feel safe, and the brain tells us the best way to feel safe is to be in control of the situation.

The issue with that is many people will actually resist someone trying to control them directly, even if it is for their betterment.

If you shove broccoli in my face, even though I know it's good for me, I will refuse to eat it. People want to make their own decisions. And they like to be in control. Through the power of indirect control, people can get far more accomplished, because people don't see that they are being forcefully influenced.

I call it the 262 rule. Two people out of ten are sweethearts! They are just the nicest people that you almost can't put in a bad mood (the thinkers). There are also two out of those ten that are just miserable, the kind that is rarely in a good mood.

However, the six left over are emotional followers. These people follow the emotional atmosphere of other people. This is powerful. For example, If you walk into a room of our imaginary ten people and say what a crappy day it is, the two negative people will continue to think negative and agree with you; the two positively minded people might not say anything but will continue to think as they usually do and that the snow looks pretty.

However, the six followers will now be negative because they're not strong internally. But if you were to go in, steeped in your core beliefs, then those six will follow you and be on the more positive side, and only the two negative people who are always negative will be the ones that are negative and therefore seem out of place.

Too often, positive people feel like the minority in our society, and this can be reversed. And even if one of the negative people wanted to chime up and say something, you are no longer a sponge that absorbed others' emotional atmospheres, and I'm willing to bet it won't put you in danger one bit.

There is no doubt that this will be tough as we all struggle with negative thoughts and the trauma that often accompanies it. Many negative thoughts will accompany change. It's one of the ways to keep you from change.

The mere mention of the word *change* can cause some people to feel uneasy. We usually find ourselves trying our best to resist change, probably because of the perceived fear or risk associated with it; more safety related negative thinking.

I want to influence your metacognitive mind and get you to think differently about being uncomfortable. I want you to think of being uncomfortable as learning. We all know we are usually not the best at things when we are learning them. That is when we typically make the most mistakes and are the most uncomfortable.

However, if you can control your thinking on this level (the same system, just repeated) and realize you're not putting yourself in danger, you will be nearly unstoppable. Just think of any professional athlete as an example and the amount of thinking involved, both conscious and subconscious!

I know we so often admire the way they handle the physical demands or bodily adjustments a runner or surfer has to make, but ultimately, we should be admiring the thought dedication it took to become a professional athlete! And not just to become one, but to have to continue to use an amazing amount of thought control, even during the sport!

But I ask of all of us to be professional thinkers! I don't really care what you actually do, how much you make, or what your title is. We all have a responsibility to be professionals in life. I am asking people to get out of their comfort zones when it is appropriate as so much brain activity happens when you are in the learning mode.

I recently attended a great storytelling event where a speaker stumbled badly. Not only that, but he also repeated his introduction twice and was bold enough to admit his stage fright. As expected, his confession was met with admiration and cheers. When he finished, the applause was loud and highly supportive. And the audience really admired his willingness to get out of his comfort zone.

Please don't mistake my intentions and put yourself in a panic situation, but I do advocate stretching one's boundaries of thought, and that can be uncomfortable.

I also like to work in this area because it's the part of life that is Godly. It's the study of the part of life God has given us control over. Remember, even though it's only partial control of the brain, it's the most crucial part. If someone is a jerk to you, you may decide not to be so vulnerable with them and even choose to take them out of your life.

But it's your decision; you choose whether or not to show your positive self and choose to redirect your energy to others who reflect the same back to you. Also, these concepts are infinite. I believe God has allowed us no limits in the emotional world; we may feast on all that is available to us.

I have yet to meet someone and have them say they see someone who is kind but they cannot be. In the world most of us live in, if someone wants to be more kind, they can. No one can see an emotional quality in someone and say they are not allowed to have it.

Only in the practical branches is this true. You cannot see someone who is taller than you and think of yourself as being taller, but you can see someone who is appreciative and think yourself actually to be a more appreciative person. This change can break through the time/space continuum and happen immediately!

Use these techniques, and as you get better at them, I am sure you will see the profound changes they will have in your life. God bless!

Helpful Lists

Negative Internal Emotional Thoughts (I am…)

Afraid	Hated
Aggravated	Unimportant
Alone	Invalidated
Anxious	Irritated
Betrayed	Inadequate
Blamed	Isolated
Confused	Lonely
Deceived	Mad
Defeated	Misunderstood
Depressed	Minimized
Deserted	Overwhelmed
Devalued	Rejected
Disappointment	Scared
Disgusting	Insecure
Dismissed	Worthless
Empty	Trapped
Fearful	Unsure
Guilty	Vulnerable
Hated	Weak
Helpless	Not good enough
Hopeless	Shameful

Positive Internal Emotional Thoughts

Emotional Toolbox

Affectionate	Grateful
Compassionate	Appreciative
Friendly	Thankful
Loving	Joyful
Sympathetic	Peaceful
Warm	Calm
Engaged	Relaxed
Helpful	Positive
Hopeful	Comfortable
Optimistic	Centered
Empowered	Content
Happy	Satisfied
Safe	Restored
Secure	Carefree
Energetic	Strong
Passionate	Powerful
Assertive	Capable
Generous	Trustworthy

Word you cannot use: *Confident*

The toolbox is the reason you're confident. Confidence is no longer centered in practical things, i.e. money, possessions, a skill, or even a relationship. These things are practical, and by rule, they can be taken away. Internal emotion cannot.

> All honor and glory to God forever and ever! He is the eternal King, the unseen one who never dies, He alone is God, Amen.
> —1 Timothy 1:17 (NLT)

WORKSHEET 2
Identifying the Specific Branches of Thought

Event

    Positive Internal Emotional

    Positive Internal Practical

    Positive External Emotional

    Positive External Practical

    Negative External Emotional

    Negative External Practical

    Negative Internal Emotional

    Negative Internal Practical

Typically, in counseling, we are dealing with situations that are considered generally negative, such as a death, trauma, or perhaps a move or an end of a relationship. Coupled with our brain first determining whether something is a threat or not, negative thoughts are usually the easiest to come up with and unfortunately the most detrimental.

However, they do need to be explored as they are the ones causing the negative emotion. Depending on the situation, different thought branches will be harder to come to. But once you become familiar with the skills and practice them, you will find that not only does it become easier, it will change everything.

About the Author

John E. Christie is a seasoned therapist with over fifteen years of experience working with people in a variety of settings, such as residential treatments centers, church settings, corporate consulting, and private practice. He holds a bachelor's degree in psychology from Western Michigan University and a master's degree in community counseling from Denver Seminary.

In addition to counseling, he also is a certified sommelier and enjoys educating people about wine. John lives with his family in Parker, Colorado, where he also has a thriving private practice.

CPSIA information can be obtained
at www.ICGtesting.com
Printed in the USA
BVHW071530150421
605029BV00008B/960

9 781098 047962